MW01066033

tell me about GOD

Written by
**Rhonda Reeves and
Jennifer Law**

Illustrated by
Timothy Robinson

**Woman's Missionary Union
Birmingham, AL 35283-0010**

Published by Woman's Missionary Union, SBC
P.O. Box 830010
Birmingham, AL 35283-0010

Dewey Decimal Classification: CE
Subject Headings: GOD (CHRISTIANITY)
                  CHILDREN'S LITERATURE

Series: Missions and Me

ISBN: 1-56309-256-5
W988104•068•05M1

Dedication

This book is dedicated to all preschoolers in hope that they will learn more about God each day of their lives.

I see the wonderful things God made.

God made the flowers,
trees, and animals.
God made the sunshine, too.

God made the moon and stars.

God made all kinds of people.

God loves everyone.

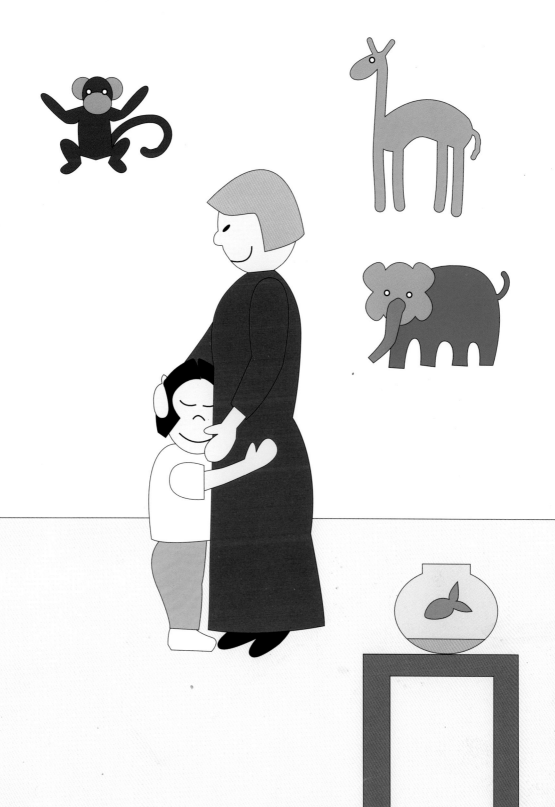

He wants us to love others.

I can talk to God.

God hears me when I pray.

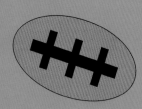

We give thanks to God

for the good things He gives us.

I love God very much. And God loves me!